Ideas in Textiles and Threads

Ideas in Textiles and Threads

Kerstin Sjödin

 VAN NOSTRAND REINHOLD COMPANY
New York   Cincinnati   Toronto   London   Melbourne

This book was originally
published in Swedish under the
title *Textila Idéer* by
I. C. A. Förlaget, Västerås, Sweden

Library of Congress Catalog Card
Number 72–1856
ISBN 0442–29960–5 cl.
ISBN 0442–29961–3 pb.

Photography – Roland Schröder

This book is set in Univers and is
printed in Great Britain by
Jolly & Barber Limited, Rugby
and bound by R. J. Acford Ltd.
Chichester, Sussex

Published by Van Nostrand
Reinhold Company, Inc.
450 West 33rd Street, New York,
N.Y. 10001 and Van Nostrand
Reinhold Company Ltd.
25–28 Buckingham Gate,
London S.W.1

Published simultaneously in
Canada by Van Nostrand
Reinhold Company Ltd.

16 15 14 13 12 11 10 9 8 7 6 5 4 3 2 1

Contents

Preface

Many people would like to do creative work with textiles in their spare time but find it difficult to get hold of patterns. This book is intended for them and for anyone else interested in textiles, as well as for schools and organizations. The materials used are carefully specified, but it is hoped that the book will stimulate ideas rather than provide them ready-made, and that it will inspire the reader to make things out of materials already available.

Kerstin Sjödin

Things it is useful to know before you start

Composition

To achieve balance in a picture, panel, etc., you have to consider the colour, shape, size and position of the motifs.

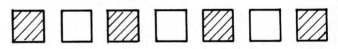

You can alternate light and dark figures.

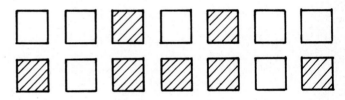

You can group or rearrange the figures to give a more dramatic note to the design.

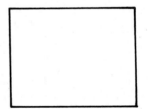

A small but interesting shape can carry as much weight as a larger, meaningless shape.

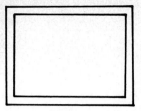

A number of small figures carry as much weight as one large one.

In general the design should be placed in the centre, though sometimes it is deliberately placed asymmetrically.

Simplification of designs

If you are not good at drawing do not attempt to draw realistically, but simplify your design as much as possible. A simplified drawing is better than a realistic one that is out of proportion.

Enlargement of designs

Even if you do not have access to any enlargement apparatus you can enlarge a design very simply. First trace or copy it on to graph paper. Then take a sheet of paper a little larger than you wish your design to be, and divide it up into as many squares as are on the graph paper. Then draw what is in each square on the graph paper in the corresponding squares on the larger sheet of paper.

Transfer of designs

The simplest way to transfer a design on to fabric is by using carbon paper, which is obtainable in various colours (choose a colour that contrasts with that of the fabric). The design can be touched up afterwards with a sharp lead pencil if it does not show up well, which may sometimes be the case with more loosely woven fabrics. Alternative methods for coarse background materials are (1) to tack or baste paper shapes which form the design on to the fabric, or (2) to draw the design on to tracing or greaseproof (wax) paper. Tack (baste) with small stitches along the design lines through paper and material and then tear away the paper. Tacking (basting) threads are removed as embroidery progresses.

Needles and pins

Blunt-pointed tapestry needles are used for all kinds of stitching over counted threads.
Sharp-pointed crewel needles are used for all kinds of free-style embroidery where threads are not counted.
Place the pins in the work at right angles to the seam. You will then be able to machine stitch the seam without removing the pins.

Mounting

Vilene (Pellon) is a non-woven material used for interlining. It is available in several different weights including an iron-on variety. Most grades are white but black is also available.

Pressing

Dampen the pressing cloth by wetting half of it, wringing it out, folding it and rolling it up with the wet half against the dry. For pressing felt do not have the cloth too wet, since felt is apt to shrink. A piece of embroidery may be lightly pressed on the wrong side; or it may be stretched tightly, right side up, with a damp cloth over it and left until the cloth is dry. Knitted and crocheted woollen articles may be lightly pressed, but do not press articles or clothes made of synthetic or mixed yarns, because they have a low melting point.

Beads

When sewing on several beads you do not need to fasten off after each one separately — the thread can easily be carried along the back, and each bead fixed down with just one or two stitches.

Sequins

Sequins are sewn on with a small bead in the centre or at the edge (wherever the hole is).

Glue and adhesives

Certain textile glues show a tendency to work through the fabric and cause marks. Try them out on a scrap of material first. Be sparing in the use of adhesive and follow the manufacturer's instructions.

Method

When the embroidery is finished and pressed, cut two pieces of iron-on Vilene (Pellon) to the measurements desired for the finished panel. Lay the embroidery wrong side up and iron on the first piece of Vilene (Pellon) absolutely straight, following the line of the weave. Turn in the edge about $\frac{3}{8}$in. and pin it down. Iron on the second piece of Vilene. Sew on metal rings if you want to hang it up.

This kind of mounting is suitable for most kinds of embroidered panels. There are many different ways of mounting embroideries, pieces of weaving, felt appliqués, etc. (Appliqué means 'applying', i.e. sewing or gluing one material on to another.) Only a few of these methods are described in this book: for mounting on chipboard (Masonite), see The Bridge Party (p. 80); for mounting in a frame see Abraham (p. 63) and Emma (p. 76).

For mounting on a wooden rod, see Tivoli (p. 64) and The Gate (p. 65).

If you are not sure which method is best for mounting a particular piece of work, it may be a comfort to know that there is no one correct way, although one method may be more suitable than another in view of the nature of the material. Any method that is practical and gives good results is correct.

Embroidery materials and threads

Many of the articles illustrated were worked in two different weights of linen thread on hand-woven linen, but there are numerous suitable alternatives. Any thread which is easily pulled through a fabric may be used for stitchery and variety of texture is obtained by using threads of different thicknesses and qualities. Thicker, rougher threads may be couched. If the article is to be washed, be sure that the colours are fast.

Abbreviations*

in.	=	inch/inches
oz.	=	ounce/ounces
yd./yds.	=	yard/yards
st.	=	stitch
k.	=	knit
p.	=	purl
ch.	=	chain
dc. / sc.	=	double crochet (UK) / single crochet (US)
htr. / hdc.	=	half treble (UK) / half double crochet (US)
tr. / dc.	=	treble (UK) / double crochet (US)
psso.	=	pass slipped stitch over: slip 1 st. knitwise, knit the next stitch and pass the slipped stitch over it.
k 2 tog.	=	knit 2 stitches together

* Where US terms differ from UK they are given in brackets.

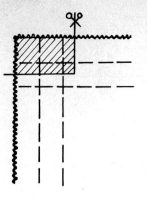
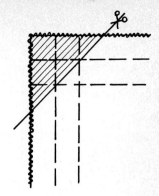

Corner stitched in sewing machine. The shaded part is cut away.

Straight corner. The shaded part is cut away.

Mitred corner. The shaded part is cut away.

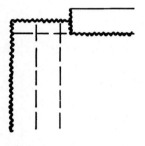
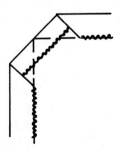
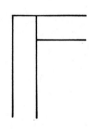

Straight corner. First fold.

Second fold.

Third and fourth folds.

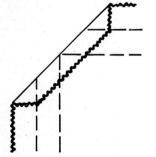

Mitred corner. First fold.

Second and third folds.

Fourth and fifth folds.

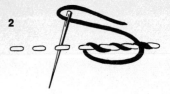

1. Running stitch, darning stitch.

2. Running stitch whipped in the same or a contrasting colour.

3. Threaded running stitch, one or two colours.

4. Two rows of running stitch threaded.
5. Back stitch.
6. Double running stitch: two rows of running stitch at right angles to each other.

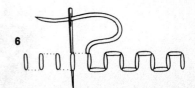

7. Pekinese stitch; a variation can also be worked on a running stitch.

8. Stem stitch, usually worked to the right.

9. Chain stitch.

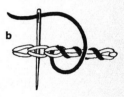

10. Whipping over (a) stem stitch or (b) chain stitch. Work the whipping in the opposite direction to the stitch.

10 a

b

11. French knots. Wind the thread round the needle, hold the thread firmly and insert the needle close to where it came up. The more times the thread is wound round, the larger the knot. May be used singly or as a filling.

11

12

12. Counted satin stitch. The stitches on the right side are parallel to the weave of the fabric.

13. Couching as an outline stitch, the thread being stitched down by hand.

13

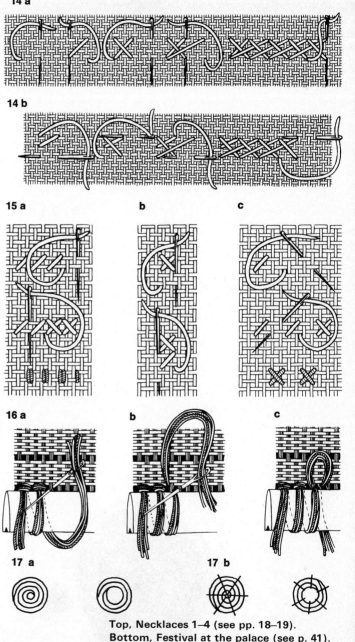

14. Long-armed or long-legged cross stitch may be worked in (a) horizontal and (b) vertical rows. The first and last stitch may, as in (b), be worked in the same direction as the other stitches. The thread must not be drawn too tightly. Best worked in a frame.

15. Cross stitch is worked over counted threads in (a) horizontal, (b) vertical rows or (c) every other stitch. It depends on how you want the back to look, or on the shape of the design. The wrong side will show either vertical or crossed stitches.

16. Rug knots are worked on a special rug base (or on tapestry canvas) with or without a gauge (a ruler would do). The loops are often cut unevenly in order to reduce the striped effect which the weaving produces.

17. Whirls. Made between the thumb and first finger (a), they are sewn down across the threads in a suitable colour (b).

14 a

14 b

15 a   **b**   **c**

16 a   **b**   **c**

17 a   **17 b**

Top, Necklaces 1–4 (see pp. 18–19).
Bottom, Festival at the palace (see p. 41).

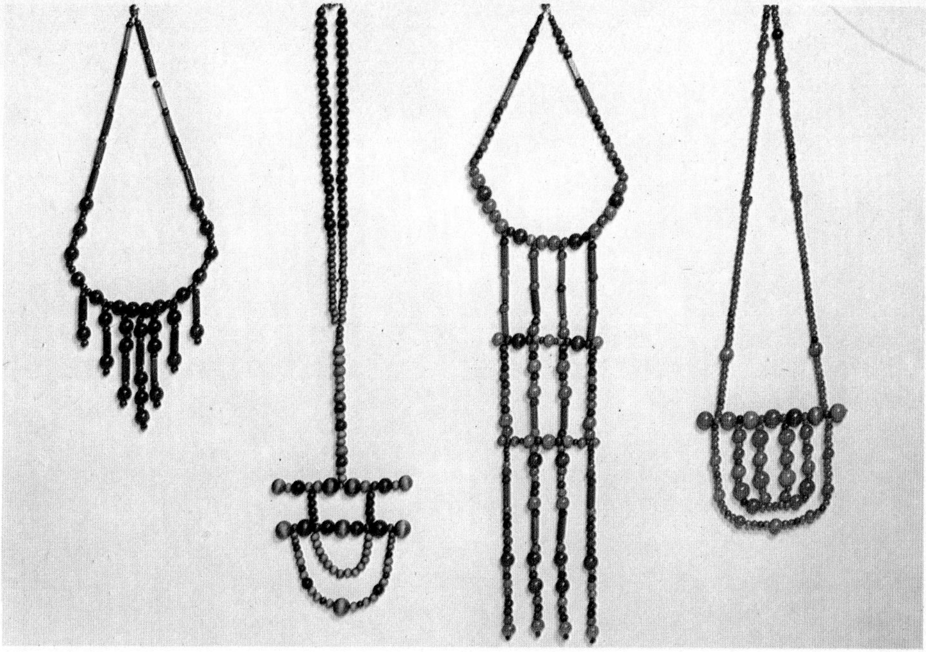

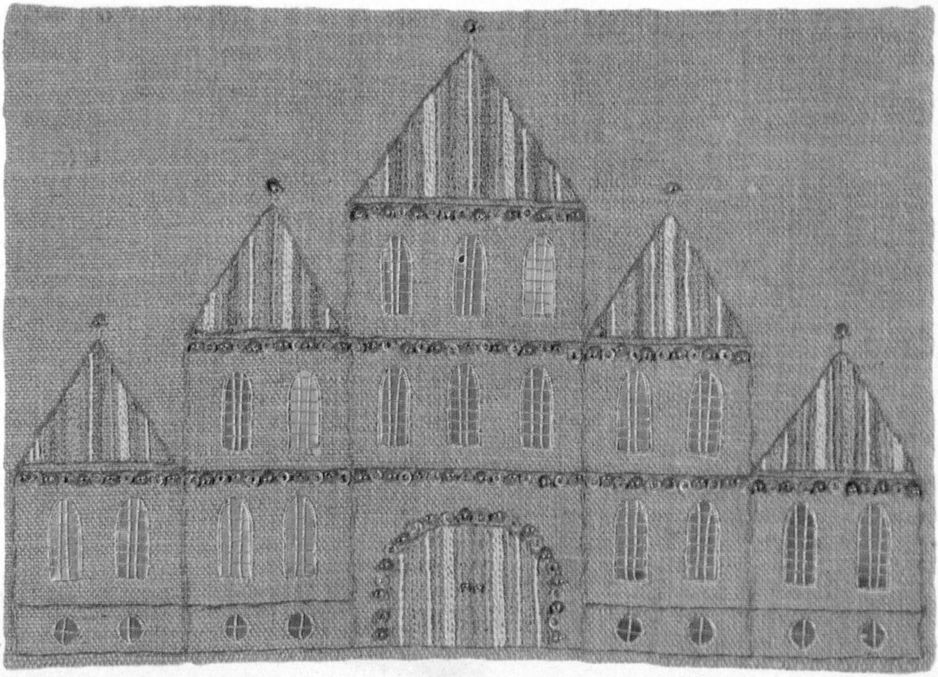

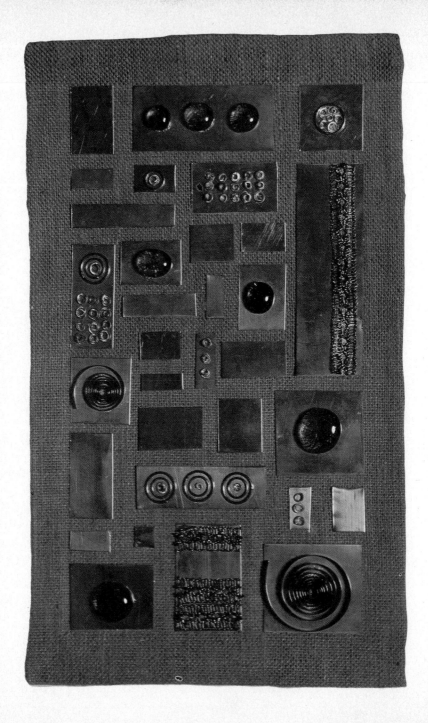

Examples

Necklace 1

MATERIALS
olive green and
turquoise dull wooden
beads
strong green thread
clasp
wire
glue

Start by attaching one half of the clasp to the thread. Thread on all the beads that go round the neck, and then attach the other half of the clasp. Fix the ends of the thread with a little glue so that they lie flat. Find the centre front, twist a length of thread double over the spot and thread the beads of the centre row on to it. A piece of wire is run through the last bead that the thread passes through before it is carried up again. Cut the wire to the desired length and bend one end so that the wooden beads cannot slip off. Before the last bead bend the other end so much that it is only just possible to get the bead on. The bottom loop is made of wire.

See colour illustration facing p. 16.

Necklace 2

MATERIALS
cerise, rose, pink, red,
orange, mauve and
beige polished wooden
beads
strong grey thread
wire
glue

The outer, bottom loop is made of wire.
See colour illustration facing p. 16.

Necklace 3

MATERIALS
polished brown
wooden beads
strong brown thread
clasp
wire
glue

The curve at the front of the neck is made of wire.
See colour illustration facing p. 16.

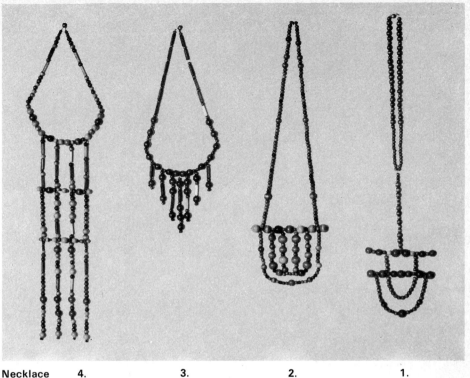

Necklace   4.   3.   2.   1.

Necklace 4

MATERIALS
beige, brown and pink
(9) dull and polished
wooden beads
strong grey thread
clasp
wire
glue

The curve at the front of the neck is made of wire.
See colour illustration facing p. 16.

Brooch

MATERIALS
framework for brooch
white fabric
white sewing thread
white and off-white
polished wooden beads
glue
pin

Cover the front of the brooch with fabric and sew beads on to it. Fasten off firmly behind. Hang three rows of beads from the brooch, threaded on to triple sewing thread. These pass through two oblong wooden beads which are glued together. (Bore holes through the beads before joining them together.) Two rows of beads are suspended from the outside ends of the oblong beads. The middle string is a continuation of the one that starts from the brooch. Fasten off the thread by passing it round the bottom bead and up again through about two beads. Fasten down the ends of the thread with glue.

Disc

MATERIALS
plastic wallpaper
shield
embroidery thread
wooden beads in
shades of cerise, red,
orange and mauve

Wind the thread round the ring and knot it behind. Then sew on the beads. The space in the middle could also be filled. Make a loop to hang it by.
See colour illustration facing p. 33.

Cushion

SIZE
11 in. × 10 in.
MATERIALS
beige cotton material
yellow, pink and red
strips
wooden beads in
yellow, pink, cerise,
red, pale brown and
pale mauve
foam rubber for
stuffing

Cut out two pieces of material the desired size for the cushion, allowing for seams. Pin and sew on the coloured bands on the right side of one half. Then lay the two pieces together with the right sides facing and sew the seams. Start just before one corner and sew three sides plus the fourth corner. Cut away any unnecessary material at the corners (see p. 13). Turn right side out and iron or press the cushion cover. Sew on the beads. Make a filling of foam rubber. For a cushion of the above measurements cut out two pieces 10¼ in. × 9¼ in., two pieces 9½ in. × 8½ in. and one piece 8¾ in. × 7¾ in. The largest pieces should be laid at the outside, the next largest inside and the smallest piece at the centre. Sew the cushion round at the edges with large stitches. Put it inside the cushion cover and sew the opening together by hand or machine. If you use the sewing machine you should sew the length of the side. Fasten off the thread by reverse-stitching in the machine.
See colour illustration facing p. 33.

The Land of Gingerbread Men

SIZE
20in. × 11in.
MATERIALS
cotton material in
shades of brown
iron-on Vilene (Pellon)

Iron Vilene (Pellon) on to the back of the ground material. This will make the material firmer to use when turning it about in the sewing machine. Cut out the figures and hearts and pin them on to the ground material. Set the machine for a very small stitch (i.e. set at 1) and the width of stitch at 4. Zigzag round the figures. When turning corners leave the needle down in the fabric, raise the presser foot and swing the material round. Finish off threads by drawing them through to the back of the work and knotting them. Press the work. Mount with Vilene (Pellon).

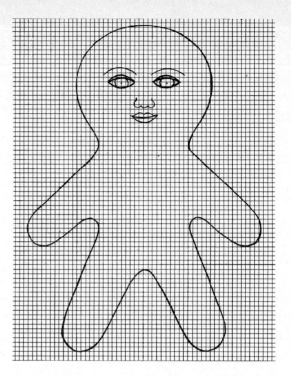

Enoch the Doll

SIZE
length 14in.
PATTERN
see diagram: one
square corresponds to
a square in a
student's notebook
MATERIALS
firm cotton fabric
thread for face
wool for hair
kapok for stuffing
STITCHES
stem stitch
satin stitch
shading stitch (long
and short stitches)

Spread out the pattern on the material folded over double with the wrong side out. Pin it. With a pencil draw round the pattern $\frac{1}{4}$in. away. Cut round this line. Remove the pins and transfer eyes, nose and mouth to one half of the doll. Embroider all the outlines in stem stitch. Work the eyes in satin stitch (see drawing) and fill in the mouth in shading stitch. Press the face from the wrong side. Lay the two halves face to face with the embroidery inwards. Pin. Sew round in the sewing machine. Start at the head and leave an opening there about 3in. long for turning. Keep the edge of the presser foot level with the outer edge of the work to keep the seam even. Snip round all the curves. Turn the doll right side out, iron it and let it cool. Start by stuffing the kapok into the legs. You will probably find it a help to use something with a blunt end to push it down. Then stuff the rest of the body, pin together and sew up the opening with double sewing thread.

You will need about 2 oz. of wool for the hair. For short hair cut lengths about 12in. long for the front, with shorter and shorter lengths as you work down towards the neck.

If you want a centre parting in the hair run a seam on the sewing machine with no. 4 stitches down the centre of the strands of wool before attaching. If you prefer a side parting, shift the seam to one side. If you want a forelock wind a little wool round two fingers, cut one side and stitch the opposite side in the sewing machine; back-stitch the lock on to the doll, using double sewing thread, then fix the end of the lock. (In back-stitching, follow the line of machine stitching.) Fasten down some of the woollen strands on the head at about the level of the eyes, so that the hair will not stand up.

Patterns for clothes may be made by adding $\frac{3}{8}$in. 'play' all round the basic pattern.

Computer

SIZE
15½in. × 9¼in.
MATERIALS
orange-coloured linen
or hessian (burlap)
sheet brass
brass rings
red and orange glass
'jewels'
springs from a broken
alarm clock
gold-coloured lace
glue
iron-on Vilene (Pellon)

Start with a piece of fabric 16¼in. × 10in. Cut out two pieces of iron-on Vilene (Pellon) the size of the finished panel. Iron one piece on to the back of the fabric. Turn in the edges all round. Pin them. Cut away any unnecessary material at the corners — as the fabric is thick, the corners may easily look clumsy otherwise. Iron on the second piece of Vilene (Pellon). Sew the metal rings for hanging the panel on to the back.

Cut the sheet brass into squares and rectangles and glue them on. If you are using lace to decorate any of these pieces, glue it on to the brass plate and turn the ends under before glueing the plate to the fabric. As you cut the edges of the brass plate, these will curl themselves up: keep these twists and glue them on with the 'jewels' and the rings.

See colour illustration facing p. 17.

Wedding

SIZE
13in. × 10in.
MATERIALS
child's drawing
close-woven, cream
linen
embroidery threads of
two different weights
iron-on Vilene (Pellon)
STITCHES
couching
stem stitch
satin stitch

This piece of embroidery uses a child's drawing as its basis. The different stitches represent the chalk lines of the original. Nothing has been added or taken away to improve the drawing.

The bride has yellow hair, pink lips and dress and an orange veil. The bridegroom has brown hair, pink lips and shirt, blue trousers and yellow shoes.

When the embroidery is finished press the work on the wrong side. Mount with iron-on Vilene (Pellon).

See colour illustration facing p. 56.

Snail

SIZE
12in. × 9½in.
MATERIALS
child's drawing
unbleached linen
brown thread — wool
or tow
iron-on Vilene (Pellon)
STITCHES
couching

Maria, aged five, has seen a snail for the first time. She is delighted with it and would like to take it home for a playmate. As she is not allowed to, she draws a snail for herself.
The snail could be enlarged before being worked. Mount with iron-on Vilene (Pellon).

Hugo the Rabbit

SIZE
9in. × 11½in.
MATERIALS
child's drawing
mauve linen or
furnishing fabric
white felt
pink linen thread
yellow, orange, cerise
and pale mauve
wooden beads
iron-on Vilene (Pellon)
glue
STITCHES
back stitch
French knots

Prepare the background first. Start with a piece of material 9¾in. × 12¼in. Cut out two pieces of iron-on Vilene (Pellon) measuring 9in. × 11½in. Iron one piece on to the back of the material. Turn in and pin down the edges. Iron on the second piece of Vilene (Pellon). Stitch round the edge in the sewing machine. Set the machine for a medium stitch (3) and keep the edge of the fabric to the edge of the presser foot to keep the seam straight. Draw the ends of thread through to the back of the work, knot them and tuck them in between the layers of material. Sew on two metal rings for hanging.

Cut out the rabbit. Embroider the eyes, nose and mouth in back stitch. Fill in the nose with French knots. Sew on the beads. Glue the rabbit on to the linen.

See colour illustration facing p. 32.

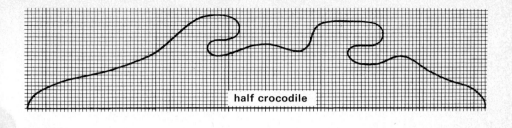

half crocodile

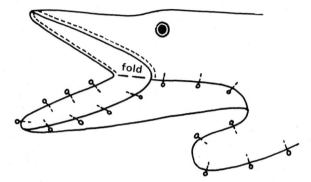

fold

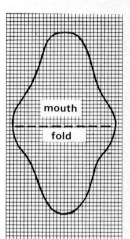

mouth

fold

Caspar the Crocodile

SIZE
9¼in. (at legs) × 24½in.
PATTERN
see diagram: one
square corresponds to
one square in a
student's notebook
MATERIALS
green and turquoise
felt glass
wooden beads in green
and turquoise
green sequins
glue
kapok, foam rubber or
rags for stuffing

Cut out two halves of the crocodile and one mouth. Work out some amusing pattern for the top half. Here a piece of turquoise felt has been cut double and decorated with small shapes in felt, beads and sequins. These are stitched on before the felt is glued down. When the top part is finished pin it to the under part. Pin in the mouth at the same time (see drawing). Sew down the upper jaw from fold to fold. Fasten off the threads by back-stitching. Then stitch the lower jaw in the same way. Finally stitch the right and left sides from the fold to a point just behind the back legs.

The crocodile may be stuffed as preferred with kapok, foam rubber or rags. Pin up the opening and stitch it in the sewing machine. The stuffed crocodile in the illustration on p. 32 was made of grey felt of the thickest quality. The design on the back was done in dark grey iron-on Vilene (Pellon) cut double. See colour illustration facing p. 40 and the front cover for the crocodile made with felt.

Hugo the Rabbit (instructions on p. 30).

Canister

SIZE
height 2½in.;
circumference 5in.
MATERIALS
empty firm cylinder
from toilet roll or
household roll
cork
pinkish mauve and
cerise felt
orange and red wooden
beads
iron-on Vilene (Pellon)
glue

Cut off the cylinder at a height of 2½in. Glue a piece of felt measuring 5in. × 2½in. round the cylinder with the join, which must be neatly made, coming at the front. Cut out a piece of felt folded double measuring 1¾in. × 2½in. (see drawing). Sew the wooden beads on to it and glue it on so as to cover the join. Draw and cut out two circles for the base in felt. Cut out another circle in iron-on Vilene (Pellon) and iron it on to one of the felt circles. Glue the two felt circles together (Vilene inside). Sew on the base with small stitches. Insert the cork.

See colour illustration facing p. 33.

Folded edge of material

Top, Memo pad (p. 39). Mirror in felt frame (p. 59).
Centre, Disc (p. 20). Cushion (p. 22).
Bottom, Lid of box (p. 69). Canister (p. 33). Box lid (p. 38).

City centre

SIZE
8in. × 13½in.
MATERIALS
beige, white and brown felt
pale mauve wooden beads
cardboard for backing
glue

Felt or another non-fraying woollen material is used for the background. Make two holes in the cardboard and thread double sewing cotton or strong thread through, so that the knots come on the side facing the felt. Cut out the motor cars the size you want. Each one can be cut out separately, varying the size and appearance to be as simple or complicated as you wish. Glue them on to the background. Sew on round beads for headlights. Glue on flat beads of the same colour for wheels. Finally glue the panel on to the cardboard.

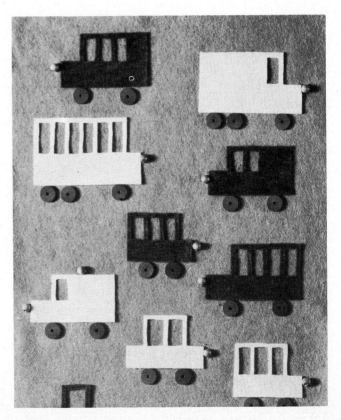

Detail of panel.

34

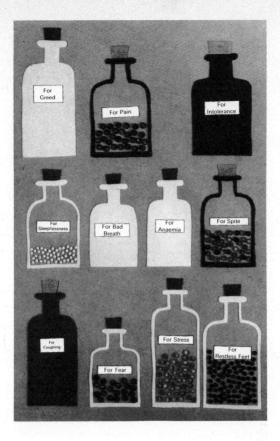

For Greed

For Pain

For Intolerance

For Sleeplessness

For Bad Breath

For Anaemia

For Spite

For Coughing

For Stress

For Fear

For Restless Feet

Home medicine chest

SIZE
10¾in. × 16½in.
MATERIALS
beige, white, dark and
light brown felt
brown, brownish
mauve, cerise, red and
white wooden beads
iron-on Vilene (Pellon)
paper labels
glue

Prepare the background first. Cut a piece of felt and two pieces of iron-on Vilene (Pellon) to the above measurements. Iron on the Vilene (Pellon) and sew on two metal rings for hanging. Cut out the bottles in white and brown felt and glue them on. Sew on the beads. Cut out corks in light and dark brown felt and glue them on. Write and glue on the labels.

See colour illustration facing p. 41.

Birds of passage

SIZE
33in. × 8in.
MATERIALS
felt and wooden beads
in blue, green and
turquoise
iron-on Vilene (Pellon)
glue

The ground material, measuring 33in. × 8in., was felt, but any other non-fraying woollen material would do. Cut one or preferably two pieces of iron-on Vilene (Pellon) the same size and iron them on to the back.

Next cut out all the birds. Cut the wings in one piece. The bodies should be high enough to cover the centre of the wings. The heads should be large enough to cover one-third of the body. Glue the head on to the body and the body on to the wings. Arrange the beads as desired and sew them on. Cut out the beaks and sew them on. Sew on the eyes. The position of the beak and eyes will determine the bird's expression. Glue the birds on to the background. A better balance will be obtained by alternating light and dark birds. Sew four metal rings on to the back for hanging.

See colour illustration facing p. 40.

Blue bird

SIZE
$7\frac{3}{4}$in. × $7\frac{3}{4}$in.
MATERIALS
light green and dark
blue felt
blue lamé
green and blue sequins
green, turquoise and
blue glass beads
metal rings
iron-on Vilene (Pellon)
glue

Cut a piece of pale green felt and two pieces of iron-on Vilene (Pellon) to the above measurements. Draw a bird on the felt and cut it out. Prepare a piece of lamé $6\frac{3}{4}$in. × $5\frac{3}{4}$in. and glue it to the back of the felt. Iron on the two layers of Vilene (Pellon) and sew on two metal rings for hanging. Cut out a beak in dark blue felt and glue it on. Buttonhole round a metal ring in double sewing thread in blue. This ring will make the eye. Sew it on and fill it up with beads. Sew beads and sequins above the head and tail. Cut out a circle $1\frac{1}{2}$in. in diameter and sew beads on to it. Glue it on.

See colour illustration facing p. 40.

Box lid

SIZE

4½in. × 4½in.

MATERIALS

cerise, orange, pink
and red felt
orange, cerise, red and
bronze glass beads
cerise wool for cord
silver lamé
foam rubber
cardboard box
glue

Start with a piece of felt 6in. square. Cut a hole with a 1½in.
diameter in the centre. Cut strips of felt of different shades
and glue them on. Sew on beads and sequins. Cut out a
ring ¼in. wide with an inside diameter of 1½in. Glue it on and
sew on beads. Glue on silver lamé or a piece of looking glass
to the back of the felt. Cut out a piece of cardboard 4⅜in.
square and round off the corners. Cut out a piece of ½in.
thick foam rubber the same size. Glue this to the cardboard
so that it will not slip. Lay the felt on top and turn in and
glue the edges. Cut off any unnecessary material at the
corners. Glue the covering on to the lid. Make a cord of
twisted wool and glue it round.

See colour illustration facing p. 33.

Memo pad

SIZE
9¼in. × 12¾in.
pad 5½in. × 8½in.
MATERIALS
pink, cerise and
orange felt
1 pink memo pad
1 pencil
cerise, orange and red
wooden beads
cardboard
glue

Cut a piece of cardboard 9¼in. × 12¾in. Cut a slit 6in. long, 2in. below the top to insert the block in. Cut out a piece of felt measuring 10½in. × 14in. and make a slit 5½in. long, 2⅝in. below the top. Glue it on to the front of the cardboard. Fold in and glue the edges on to the back. Slip the back of the pad through the slit and if necessary glue it on to the back. Cut out a piece of felt 8¾in. × 12½in. for the back and sew two metal rings on the top corners for hanging. Glue the felt on to the cardboard. Decorate the front with felt and beads, sewing on the beads before glueing on the pieces of felt. Sew on a piece of felt 1½in. × 1¼in. at the bottom with six beads to hold the pencil. To make sure the hole is the right size pin the felt first over the pencil with two pins, then remove the pencil and sew the felt on to the larger piece of felt, which is then glued on to the panel.

See colour illustration facing p. 33.

Leather mittens

PATTERN
see diagram: one
square corresponds to
a square in a
student's notebook
MATERIALS
pieces of leather
linen thread
wooden beads in
cerise, red and mauve
STITCH
couching

As the pieces of leather are usually small, one generally has to do a good deal of joining to produce a pair of mittens. Joins may be made either by hand or in a swing-needle sewing machine (for length of stitch use 2, width of stitch 4). Of course, the leather can be bought in larger pieces but the mittens will then work out considerably more expensive. The couching is done with linen thread and ordinary sewing thread. Sew the beads on last.

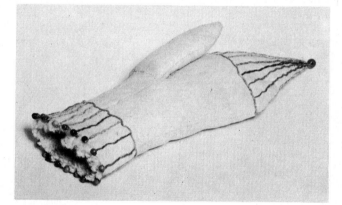

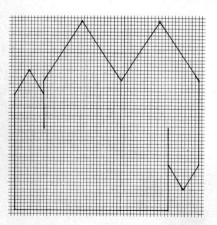

Tea or coffee cosy for Christmas (p. 44). Caspar the Crocodile (p. 31). Blue bird (p. 37). Birds of passage (p. 36).

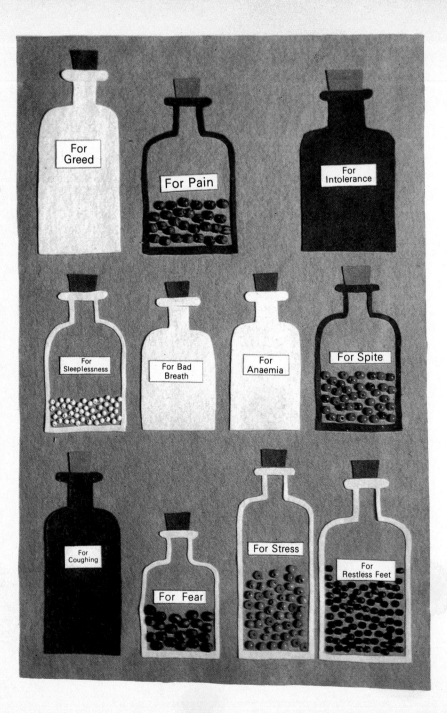

Festival at the palace

SIZE
14½in. × 10in.
MATERIALS
medium or heavy-
weight green linen
embroidery threads in
three shades of green
gold thread
sheet brass
bronze-coloured beads
and sequins
iron-on Vilene (Pellon)
glue
STITCHES
chain stitch
couching

Start with a piece of linen 15¼in. × 10¾in. Oversew the edges in a swing-needle sewing machine. Iron the Vilene (Pellon) on to the back. Transfer the pattern on to the linen. Couch round the outlines. Double thread was used here as the thread was thin. Work the roof and door in chain stitch. Sew on the sequins, beads and brass shavings obtained by cutting along the very edge of the sheet. Cut out the windows in sheet brass and glue them on. Stretch gold thread across them to form panes. Lay gold thread round the windows and sew it down. Turn back and pin a margin of ¾in. all round and lay the panel upside down on a soft surface. Iron on another layer of Vilene (Pellon). Sew on two metal rings for hanging.

See colour illustration facing p. 16.

Home medicine chest (instructions on p. 35).

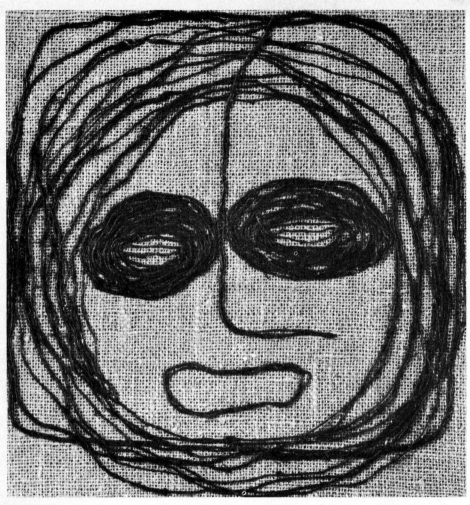

Ugly mask

SIZE
9¼in. × 9¼in.
MATERIALS
natural linen or hessian
(burlap)
brown wool, linen
thread or weaving yarn
iron-on Vilene (Pellon)
STITCH
couching

The point of interest here is the way the thread is laid. This is probably the easiest way to portray a face, mask, etc. Sometimes a single thread is used, sometimes two are couched together. It is best to have a sketch to work from. Vilene (Pellon) mounting.

42

Royal consorts

SIZE
17¼in. × 11½in.
MATERIALS
brown hessian (burlap)
linen or cotton
weaving thread or
string
gold cord
STITCH
couching

When the design has been worked and the threads drawn back to the wrong side and fastened off, cut another piece of fabric the same size for the back. Lay the two pieces together with the right sides facing and stitch three sides. Leave an opening at the bottom but stitch all the corners in the sewing machine as it is easier to keep them neat. Cut away any unnecessary material at the corners (see p. 13). Turn inside out and press. Sew up the opening. Sew three metal rings on the back for hanging.

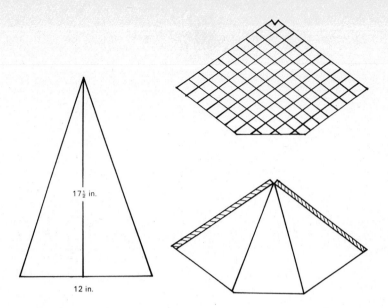

17½ in.

12 in.

Tea or coffee cosy for Christmas

SIZE
17½in. high with a
12in. base (see fig. 1)
MATERIALS
green easily-
laundered material
e.g. a non-iron
synthetic
iron-on Vilene (Pellon)
foam rubber
green and blue glass
and wooden beads

Cut out three triangles allowing ⅜in. for a seam. Cut out three pieces of iron-on Vilene (Pellon) the same size and iron on to the back. Decorate the triangles. Lay two pieces with the right sides together, pin one of the long sides and stitch in the sewing machine, leaving ⅜in. open at the top. (The pins can be placed to mark the ⅜in. turning reverse stitch at beginning and end.) Pin on the third piece and sew on both sides. Cut away any unnecessary turnings at the top. Press the seams lightly. Turn the work inside out. Cut out a strip of the green material 16in. long by ¾in. wide and turn in the raw edges. Sew it together with invisible stitches. Twist it to make four loops and sew it to the top of the cosy. Cut out three pieces of foam rubber and three pieces of Vilene (Pellon), using the same pattern but omitting the margin for seams. Iron the Vilene (Pellon) on. Lay all three pieces of foam rubber side by side and cut out a lining of the green material allowing ⅜in. for turning at the outside edges of the triangles (see fig. 2). Lay the material over the foam rubber

with the Vilene (Pellon) at the bottom. Work a pattern with large stitches on the sewing machine (e.g. diamond pattern, see fig. 3). Pin and sew up the sides where a margin has been left. Insert the inner pyramid into the outer one. Turn in and pin the $\frac{3}{8}$in. wide hem at the bottom, sewing it by machine if preferred.

See colour illustration facing p. 40.

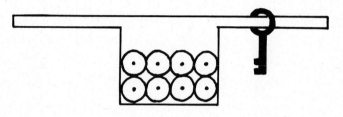

Christmas gnomes

SIZE
height 4½in. (without cap)
MATERIALS
firm empty cylinder from toilet roll or household roll
red felt scraps of fur
leftovers of red yarn
suitcase keys
cotton material for bag
glue

Cut out a piece of felt 4½in. wide and 6in. long. Glue or stitch on pieces of felt with wooden beads on them. Bear in mind in glueing on the beads that the join must come at the centre front. Glue the felt on to the cylinder. Prepare the fur for the face and beard, using a razor to cut away the hair from the face or using a smooth leather there. Draw in the eyes and mouth with india ink. After gluing on the face and beard, make the cap. This may be either knitted or crocheted, and may well be rather on the large side. If you want to make a household gnome, only the apron measuring 2in. × 1¾in. needs bead ornamentation. Hang the key on the band which is in one piece with the apron (see drawing). The band is glued down at the centre of the back.

Stitch the bag on the wrong side and make a hem 1¼in. wide at the top. Fill the sack with lavender or cotton wool and tie it round with a cord.

See colour illustration facing p. 48.

Christmas tree

SIZE
10¾in. × 17¼in.
MATERIALS
white, pink and red felt
sequins, glass and
wooden beads in
yellow, orange, pink,
cerise, red and lilac
iron-on Vilene (Pellon)
glue

Iron a piece of Vilene (Pellon) of the same size to the back of the white felt which measures 10¾in. × 17¼in. Sew on two metal rings for hanging. Cut out two Christmas trees, one in pink and one in red. Cut about twenty strips out of the darker tree and glue them on to the lighter one to represent branches. Cut long strips ¼in. wide into shorter lengths, rounding them off at one end, to represent the trunk and roots of the tree. Sew all beads and sequins on to the tree before glueing it to the background material. Glue on the trunk and roots. Sew on some sequins and beads to form the star at the top, and sew others by the side of the tree and down at the base, using thread the same colour as the beads.

See colour illustration.

Gnomes (instructions p. 46). Christmas tree (p. 48).

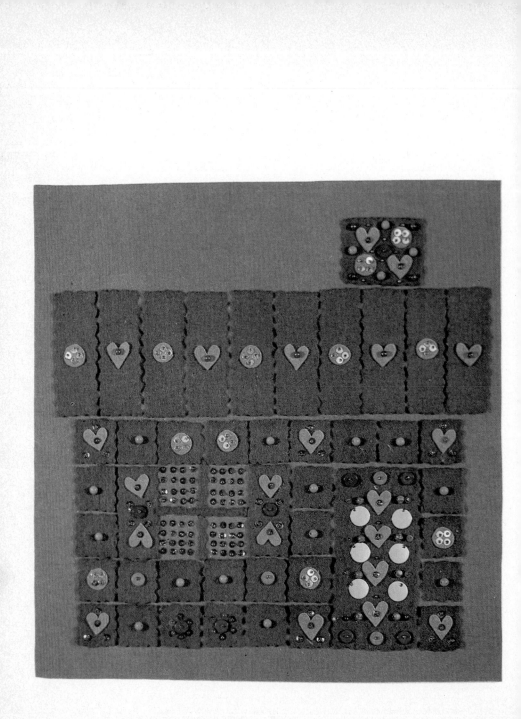

Gingerbread house

SIZE
14½in. × 15¼in.
MATERIALS
mauve, dark and light
brown felt
mauve and brown
speckled wooden beads
silvery pink, blue and
mauve sequins
bronze beads
iron-on Vilene (Pellon)
glue

Prepare the background first. Iron Vilene (Pellon) on to the back. Sew on two metal rings for hanging. Cut ten strips 1⅜in. wide and 4⅛in. long. These are to form the roof, but first the edges must be shaped, after which they will be 1¼in. × 4in. To shape the edges, move the material from side to side keeping the scissors still. Practise on paper first. Do the same with the other pieces. The door when finished is 2½in. × 5½in., the window bars two strips of 1¼in. and one of 2½in. and the other pieces about 1¼in. × 1¼in., often narrower than 1¼in. Cut out rounds and hearts in the light brown felt. Sew on all the beads and sequins. Glue the pieces on to the background. Sew sequins on to the window panes.

See colour illustration opposite.

Gingerbread house (instructions above).

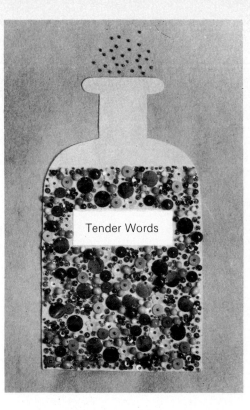

Tender Words

Tender words

SIZE
8¾in. × 13½in.

MATERIALS
beige and champagne-
coloured felt
yellow, orange, pink,
cerise, red and mauve
wooden beads
silvery pink,
gold-coloured, yellow,
orange, pink, cerise
and red sequins
red glass beads
bronze-coloured beads
iron-on Vilene (Pellon)
glue
paper label

Cut a piece of felt 8¾in. × 13½in. Iron Vilene (Pellon) on to the back and sew on two metal rings for hanging. Cut out a bottle in the champagne-coloured felt. Sew the beads and sequins on to it. Leave a space for the label. Glue the bottle on to the base. Sew on the beads above the neck of the bottle. Write the label and glue it on.

See colour illustration facing p. 57.

Bruno the Elephant

SIZE
height 6in., 10½in.
round body
MATERIALS
2 oz. thick grey wool
set of 4 knitting
needles pointed at both
ends, size 7 (6)
crochet hook no. 5 mm
(H/8)
pink felt for soles of
feet
pink wooden beads for
eyes
kapok for stuffing

Body

Knitting Instructions: Cast on 36 stitches; divide them evenly on three needles. Knit 28 rows. Then start reducing. Slip 1 stitch and knit 1, pass the slipped stitch over the knitted one (psso). Knit 8, knit the last two stitches on the needle together. Work the other two needles the same way. Continue reducing in the same way until 4 stitches remain on each needle. Knit one row without reducing. Break off the wool, thread all the stitches on to it and fasten it but do not cut it off. Thread through another length of wool and pull it until both ends are the same length. Plait (braid) the three strands of wool to make a tail about 2in. long, knotting it at the end. Cut off the ends.

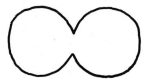

Ears

Crochet Instructions: Start with a ring of 5 chain stitches and work into the top loop of the stitches. Work half trebles (half double crochet) for the first row, after that half treble (half double crochet) into every other stitch. When the work measures $2\frac{1}{2}$in. in diameter break off the wool and draw it through the last loop. Fasten off the end you started with, but leave the end thread to stitch the ear on to the body. Work a second ear in the same way.

Legs

Crochet Instructions: Make 22 chain stitches. Work dc (sc) into the back loop of the stitch, for 8 rows. Break off and draw the wool through the last stitch. Sew the leg up and then with the same wool work a line in back stitch through the two layers so as to form two legs. Fasten off the wool. Work two more legs in the same way.

Press the body and ears if necessary. Stuff the body and legs with kapok. Cut out soles for the feet (see drawing) and sew them on with pink thread. Do not sew the legs and ears on to the body until the trunk is finished.

Trunk

Crochet Instructions: Pick up 33 stitches round the opening of the body. Work 2 rows in dc (sc). Start decreasing from row 3. Decrease 11 stitches in the first decreasing row by skipping over every 3rd stitch. Next row skip over every 5th stitch. In the third decreasing row skip over every 6th stitch. There will now be 15 stitches left. Skip over every 3rd stitch in the next row, then over every 5th in the next row. Work 4 rows decreasing only 1 stitch in each row. Work 30 rows without decreasing. Decrease 1 stitch in the last row. The last 6 rows are worked into the front loop of the stitch. All the other rows into the two loops. Break off the wool.

Horace the Horse

SIZE
height 9–11 in.;
length 9¼ in.;
14½ in. round body
MATERIALS
about 4 oz. thick blue
wool
five needles pointed at
both ends, no. 7 (6)

Body

Knitting Instructions: Cast on 48 stitches. Divide them on to four needles. Knit 38 rows. Then work reducing rows alternating with knitted rows (see drawing p. 54). Break off the wool, draw it through the stitches and fasten off. Make a tassel for the tail and sew it on.

Neck

crochet hook no. 5 mm (H/8)
dark blue felt for soles of feet and ears
orange and medium blue felt
gold braid
pink, orange and blue cotton yarn for saddle cloth
dark blue leather for bridle
dark blue wooden beads for eyes
kapok for stuffing

Knitting Instructions: Cast on 24 stitches and work in rib, 1 k 1 p, for 23 rows. Cast off. Fasten off the wool.

Legs

Crochet Instructions: Make a chain of 13 stitches. Work one row dc (sc) and then 5 rows tr (dc). Break off the wool and sew the leg up. Make three more legs.

Chest

Crochet Instructions: Start with a ring of 5 chain. Work 6 rows dc (sc). Increase the number of stitches by 7 each row. Break off the wool and draw through the last stitch. Leave the end for sewing on.

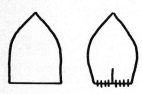

Head

Crochet Instructions: Make a chain of 20 stitches. Work 10 rows dc (sc), working into both loops of the stitch. Reduce in the following four rows by skipping over every 3rd stitch. Fasten off. Turn the head inside out.

Press the pieces lightly if necessary and stuff them with kapok. Cut out ovals for the soles of the feet and sew them on. Sew on the parts of the body. Cut out ears in felt. Make a small fold in the ear when sewing it on (see drawing). Make a bridle out of strips of leather. The saddlecloth is 4½in. × 8½in. and the embroidery on it is couched. The gold braid and pieces of felt round the edge are sewn on.

See colour illustration facing p. 56.

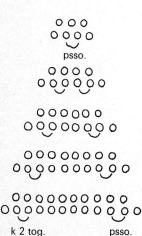

psso.

k 2 tog.   psso.

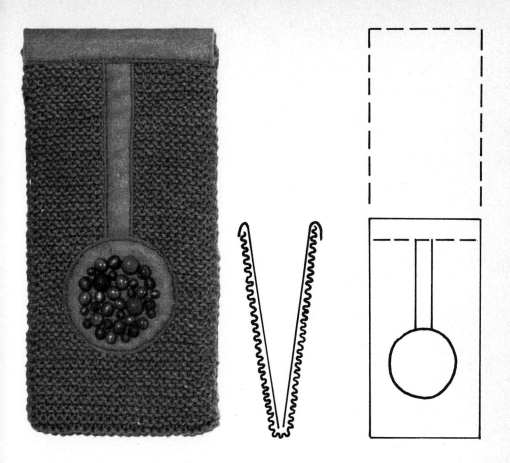

Knitted green spectacle case

SIZE
3⅝in. × 6¾in.
MATERIALS
green cotton yarn
knitting needles
size 11 (2)
turquoise felt
blue and turquoise
wooden beads
iron-on Vilene (Pellon)

Knitting Instructions: Cast on 24 stitches. Work in garter stitch. When the work is 13½in. long, cast off and finish off the ends. Cut out the pieces of felt, first a strip a good ½in. wide and 10¾in. long. Cut this into two pieces 4in. and 6¾in. long respectively. Cut out a round a good 2in. in diameter and two pieces 3⅜in. wide and 7⅜in. long. Sew the shorter strip and the round on to the front of the case by machine. Then sew the longer piece on to the back. Sew on the beads. Iron two layers of Vilene (Pellon) on to the back of the large pieces of felt. These will make both the top edge and the lining. Pin down one end of the felt ⅜in. from the top edge (see drawing) and sew it down. Fasten off the threads by drawing them through and knotting them at the back. Sew down the edge of the other half of the lining in the same way. Fasten the felt to the inside with a few stitches. Sew the case together from the right side with the same yarn as it was knitted with.

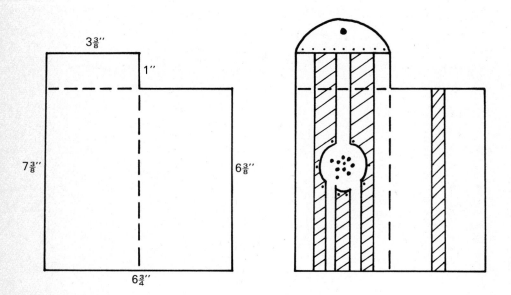

Knitted grey spectacle case

SIZE
3⅜in. × 6⅜in.
MATERIALS
chenille yarn in
beige-grey
no. 11 (2) knitting
needles
black felt or leather
black glass beads
press stud
iron-on Vilene (Pellon)

Knitting Instructions: As chenille yarn is sometimes difficult to obtain, the number of stitches will not be given. Instead, knit a sample with the yarn to be used and work according to the diagram. Fasten off the threads. Prepare the pieces for the decoration and the lining (see drawing). The lining pieces are 3¼in. × 6in. Iron two layers of Vilene (Pellon) on to the back, and also on to the back of the two pieces that form the flap. Sew one half of a press stud on to the flap and sew on all the pieces of felt by hand. Sew on the

Horace the Horse (instructions on p. 53). Wedding (p. 28).

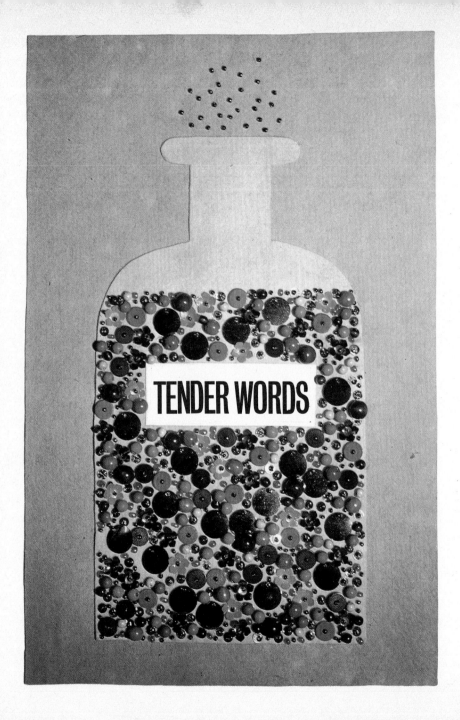

beads and the other half of the press stud. Fix the lining with a few stitches. Sew the case together by hand with the same yarn that it was knitted with.

Tender words (instructions on p. 50).

Pocket mirror

SIZE
2¾in. × 5¼in.
MATERIALS
mirror
closely-woven orange
linen
embroidery threads in
cerise, orange and red
gold thread
STITCHES
stars
whirls

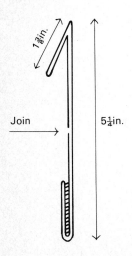

1⅜in.

Join

5¼in.

The shape of the mirror must be considered in determining the size of the embroidered areas. For a mirror of the size given here cut a piece of linen measuring 4in. × 16in.; i.e., 2¾in. + 1¼in. (width of hems) = 4in.; 1⅜in. + 1⅜in. (the embroidered areas) + 5¼in. (back) × 2 = 16in. (see drawing).

Overcast the linen all round either by hand or machine. Fold it in half so that the join, which must be neat, falls at the back of the mirror. Stitch it lightly together. Measure out and tack (baste) the two rectangles of 2¾in. × 1⅜in. at each end. Working through only one thickness of fabric, embroider stars by setting four stitches so that they cross one another. Tie them down with a short stitch at the centre. Make whirls, some with and some without a hole at the centre, and sew them down with a suitably coloured thread. Turn in ⅝in. along the long edges at top and bottom. Turn over the embroidered panels, following the line of the weave, and sew the edges together at the right-hand side. Insert the mirror and sew the edges together on the other side and along top and bottom. Make a cord about 18in. long of the seam thread as was used for the embroidery. The join in the cord should come just beside a patch of embroidery. Whip the cord on, the stitches following the direction of the twist.

See colour illustration facing p. 64.

Mirror with felt frame

SIZE
7½in. × 10½in.
MATERIALS
cerise and champagne-coloured felt
mirror 4¾in. in diameter
gold thread
crochet hook no. 5 mm (H/8)
cerise and orange wooden beads
cardboard
glue
STITCHES
couching
chain

Cut out two pieces of cardboard to the above measurements. Crochet twenty lengths of chain stitches, each 7½in. long, in gold thread. Couch them down on to the champagne-coloured piece of felt which measures 7½in. × 10½in. Glue this on to one of the pieces of cardboard. Cut strips of the cerise-coloured felt and sew beads on to them. The strips at the bottom and round the mirror are ½in. wide, the one at the top is 1½in. wide and those at the sides, 1¼in. (These latter turn over the edge and are glued down at the back: only about ½in. is visible at the front.) Glue on all the strips and the mirror. Prepare a piece of champagne-coloured felt measuring 8¾in. × 10½in. Sew on two brass rings for hanging. Glue this felt on to the other piece of cardboard. Turn in and glue the hems along the sides. Glue the two pieces of cardboard together. Lastly, glue the cerise-coloured felt strips from the front edges down at the back.

See colour illustration facing p. 33.

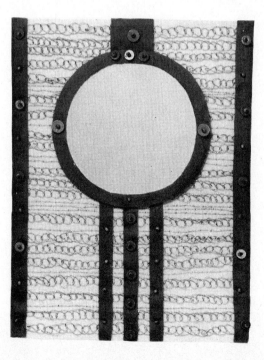

Mirror in Thai silk

SIZE
8½in. × 12½in.
(short sides,
8½in. × 3¼in.)
MATERIALS
mauve Thai silk
mirror
mauve felt
brownish-mauve silk
for cord
bronze coloured beads
iron-on Vilene (Pellon)
cardboard
glue

Iron a piece of Vilene (Pellon) measuring 11¼in. × 20in. on to a piece of silk the same size. Turn in ¼in. all the way round. Measure out and tack the short sides according to the measurements. Then measure a point along one of the short sides that is equidistant from the edges in both directions, and cut a round hole 1⅜in. in diameter. Overcast the edge. Cut out two rings in felt, 2in. in diameter and with a hole 1¼in. across. Sew one to the back and one to the front with small stitches. Cover the stitches with a cord. Cut out two circles in felt 1in. in diameter and sew beads on them. Glue them on. Sew on the other beads. Do the same with the other short side. Then cut out a piece of cardboard measuring 8½in. × 12½in. and glue it on to a piece of mirror the same size. Lay the cardboard with the mirror on to the inside of the material and turn the edges over it. Glue down the long sides. Spread a little glue round the back of the holes and press these areas on to the mirror. If necessary, cut away a little of the turn-in on the short sides. Sew up the short sides with small stitches. Sew two metal rings on to the back for hanging.
See colour illustration facing p. 72.

Square mirror

SIZE
11in. × 11in.
MATERIALS
greyish-brown linen
sewing thread
sewing silk or
machine embroidery
thread in shades of
pink and cerise
silver thread
cord of linen thread
silver sequins
pink and brownish-
mauve glass beads
iron-on Vilene (Pellon)
cardboard
glue
STITCH
darning on sewing
machine

Cut out two similar pieces of linen measuring 12in. × 12in. Overcast the edges in the sewing machine. Iron Vilene (Pellon) on to the backs. Stitch the outlines of the pattern in the sewing machine: two squares and twelve horseshoe shapes on one of the pieces of linen. Fill in the figures in darning stitch worked on the sewing machine. Practise on a scrap of material first. Work round the edges in silver thread. Lay and pin down a piece of linen 8in. × 8in. in the centre. Working from the back, sew round the outline of the inner square. Cut away the material in the centre and mitre the corners. Turn the work to the wrong side and press the opening. Lay the two large pieces of linen together with the right sides inside and pin the edges. Sew up three sides. Cut away any unnecessary material at the corners, turn the work inside out and press. Sew on sequins and beads. Sew two metal rings on to the back for hanging. Cut a piece of cardboard 10¾in. × 10¾in. and glue the mirror, which is the same size, on to it. Insert the cardboard with the mirror and sew up the fourth side.

See colour illustration facing p. 72.

Mirror in furnishing fabric

SIZE
11¼in. × 20in.
MATERIALS
brown speckled
furnishing fabric
brown cotton material
for back
mirrors
felt
wooden beads in
shades of mauve
bronze-coloured beads
cardboard
glue

Cut a piece of furnishing fabric 12¾in. × 21½in. Cut a piece of cotton material 12¼in. × 21⅛in. Order two mirrors in a glass shop, one 5in. × 5in. and one 1⅜in. in diameter. If you have a glass-cutter at home you can easily cut a small piece of mirror yourself. It need not be round, as the felt will cover the edges. Cut strips of the light-coloured felt and glue them on to the furnishing fabric. Sew on the beads. Cut out a square of the dark felt 6in. × 6in. and glue it on. Sew beads on the pieces of felt that will cover the edges of the mirrors. Glue them on to the respective mirrors. Cut out two pieces of cardboard, one 11¼in. × 20in. and the other 10¾in. × 19⅝in. for the back. Lay the furnishing material right side up over the larger piece of cardboard, turn in and glue down the edges at the back. Do the same with the piece of brown cotton material and the smaller piece of cardboard. Lay these two pieces back to back and sew up the edges by hand or glue together. Sew two metal rings on to the back for hanging. Glue on the mirrors.

Abraham

SIZE
13¼in. × 14½in.
with frame
MATERIALS
unbleached linen or
linen scrim
linen thread or wool
string
STITCH
couching

Oversew the edges of the linen in a close zigzag on a swing-needle machine. The different threads and cords are couched. Order a frame from a picture framer's and plane it down at the back so that it will not be too thick. Insert tough paper, fitting it to the corners and gluing it down at the back. Finally run a cord alternately through the edge of the material and round the frame.

Tivoli

SIZE
12½in. × 11¾in.
MATERIALS
yellowish-brown linen
and thread
embroidery threads in
orange, red, cerise and
mauve
wooden rod
STITCHES
couching
whirls

Hem the material top and bottom. Make a cord 22in. long of yellowish-brown linen thread to match the fabric. Sew it on to the back, leaving loops to run a rod through for hanging (see drawing). Transfer the pattern to the material using carbon paper. Embroider. Press the work. Run the rod through.

See colour illustration opposite.

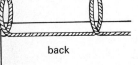

back

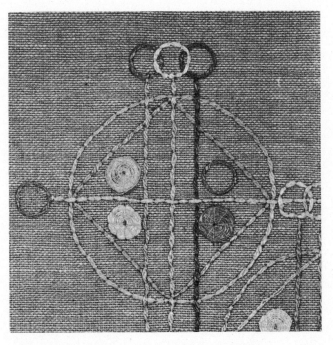

Detail of embroidery.

Top, left, Pencil case (instructions on p. 72). Top, right, Pocket mirror (p. 58). Bottom, Tivoli (p. 64).

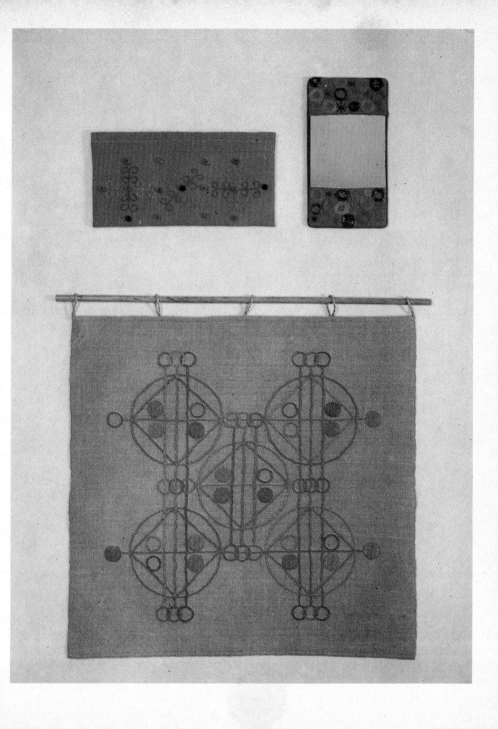

Gate

SIZE
9¼in. × 6½in.
MATERIALS
grey even-weave linen
black linen
thread
wooden rod
STITCHES
stem stitch
satin stitch

Draw the pattern on squared paper, allowing two, four or six threads to each square. In this way you can make the gate whatever size you wish. Embroider the outlines in stem stitch and the rest in satin stitch. Hem the sides and run a rod through at the top. Make a cord or sew two metal rings on to the back for hanging.

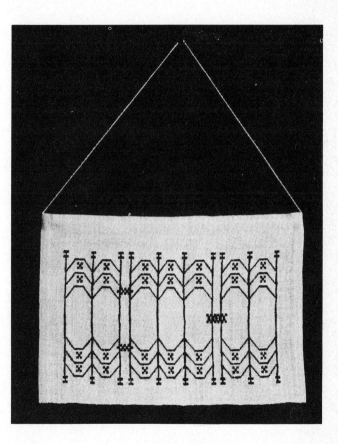

Emma (instructions on p. 76).

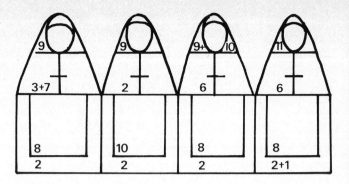

Old folk

SIZE
12in. × 6in.
MATERIALS
medium-weight
unbleached linen scrim
embroidery threads in
orange, cerise, red and
mauve, in two
different weights
iron-on Vilene (Pellon)
STITCHES*
1. stem stitch
2. long-armed cross
   stitch
3. cross stitch
4. chain stitch
5. whipped stem
   stitch
6. satin stitch
7. back stitch
8. Pekinese stitch
9. French knots
10. lazy daisy
    (detached chain)
    stitch
11. couching flowers
*The numbers refer to
the above diagram.

Overcast the edge of the linen in the sewing machine or by hand. Transfer the pattern to the linen using carbon paper. Then iron Vilene (Pellon) to the back. The size of the piece of Vilene (Pellon) will be the size of the panel when completed. Vilene (Pellon) is particularly helpful if the linen is an open weave, as otherwise the threads are inclined to pull when embroidered in free style.

Begin by working the outlines in stem stitch. Then fill the figures in (see diagram above for a general guide to stitches). The hair is worked in long stitches with a stitch across the middle to keep them in place. The eyes and buttons are done with French knots. The mouth is worked in chain stitch. The centre line in front and the line of the sleeves is worked in whipped stem stitch or chain stitch. The hair, mouths and aprons are worked with one type of thread, the rest with a different weight.

When the work is finished press it lightly from the wrong side or lay a damp cloth over it. Mount with Vilene (Pellon).

See colour illustration on the front cover.

Detail of panel.

Ladies of Holland

SIZE
15¾in. × 15¾in.
MATERIALS
red, black and white
linen
embroidery threads in
cerise, orange, red,
mauve and green
lace-making or other
fine twisted thread
iron-on Vilene (Pellon)
chipboard (Masonite)
STITCHES
appliqué
couching
running stitch
French knots

Cut out four halves of skirts, two bodices and two caps in iron-on Vilene (Pellon). Iron these pieces on to the black and white linen as applicable. Try to keep them in line with the weave of the fabric. Allow for turnings. Turn in the raw edges and tack (baste) the pieces on to the red linen, again keeping to the line of the weave. Sew them on. Embroider the shoes in running stitch with two threads of different shades of orange.

The aprons are worked in couching using stripes of orange, red and mauve. The tulips are made of between five and seven long stitches, the stalks of one and the leaves of two stitches. For the flowers themselves two threads of different shades were used; for the stalks and leaves three, two of which were of one type of thread and the other of a different weight. The front inlet is worked in French knots and couching, the knots being in the same shades as the aprons. The caps are of linen with lace-making thread couched on in a wavy line and sewn down with sewing thread.

For pressing and mounting, see The Bridge Party (p. 80).

Box lid

SIZE
5¼in. in diameter
(¼in. larger than the box)
MATERIALS
mauve and cerise linen
wooden beads in
mauve, cerise, pink,
orange and red
cardboard
iron-on Vilene (Pellon)
STITCH
appliqué

Cut out two circles in cardboard, one 5¼in. and one 5in. in diameter. Then cut two circles in linen, one 6in. and one 5¾in. in diameter. Overcast the edge of the linen either by sewing machine or by hand. Embroider the larger piece. In the present case the centre piece, measuring 1¾in. × 1¾in. plus hem, is sewn on with small stitches. Sew on the beads. Stretch the pieces of linen over the appropriate pieces of cardboard (see figs. 1 and 2). Prepare a strip of linen 2¼in. wide and 17¼in. long. Cut a strip of Vilene (Pellon), 1⅝in. wide and 16½in. long and iron it on. Leave ⅜in. turning at each end and along one side and ¼in. along the other side.

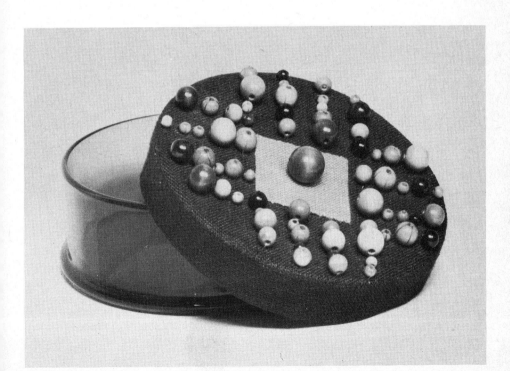

Fold the strip in half lengthwise. Turn in the hems (see fig. 3). Sew the strip to the inner round (see fig. 4). Sew the ends together. Sew it to the outer circle (see fig. 5). If you take small stitches using thread of exactly the same shade as the linen, there will be no need to cover the seam. If you do wish to cover it, you can do so with a cord.

See colour illustration facing p. 33.

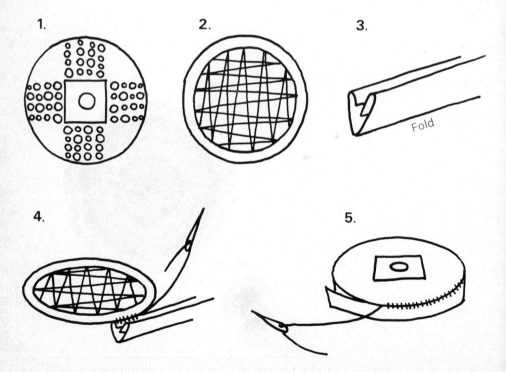

1.

2.

3.

Fold

4.

5.

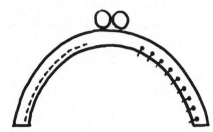

Purse

SIZE
3½in. × 5¼in.
MATERIALS
ochre-coloured linen
cotton material or
taffeta in the same
shade for lining
pale brick red linen
for appliqué
cotton and linen
threads in various
shades of pink
silver thread
silvery frame
STITCHES
buttonhole
couching
back stitch

The size and shape of the purse must be governed by the shape of the frame. Make a paper pattern. Cut out four pieces, two in linen and two in the lining material, allowing ⅜in. all round for a hem. Overcast the edge of the piece of linen to be embroidered. Embroider it. Here the piece appliquéd on at the centre is embroidered in back stitch in pink and silver. Sew this piece on with buttonhole stitch. Cover the seam with couching. When the embroidery is finished, press the work lightly from the wrong side. Pin together one of the pieces of linen and one piece of lining with the right sides facing. Sew round in the sewing machine, leaving an opening at the top. Cut away any unnecessary material. Turn inside out. Sew the opening together and if necessary press lightly. Do the same with the two other pieces. Open the frame and sew the two sides of the purse on to it. Finally sew these together with small stitches. The seam may then be covered with a cord. This kind of mounting requires a relatively wide frame, as otherwise the purse will be too small. If the holes in the frame are placed close together you can easily sew the purse on in back stitch. If the holes are placed further apart it is better to sew it on by the edges.

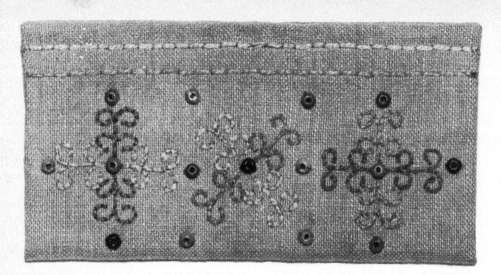

Pencil case

SIZE
6½in. × 3¼in.
(for short pencils)
MATERIALS
orange linen or
linen mixture
red vinyl
red Velcro fastener,
⅝in. wide
embroidery thread and
wooden beads in
cerise, orange and red

Start with a piece of material 7⅛in. × 13in., = (6½in. + ⅝in. hem allowance) × (4 × 3¼in.). If you use linen, iron on a piece of Vilene (Pellon) 6½in. × 6½in. first (see fig. 1a). Fold the strip in half crosswise and sew it together with a few stitches (see fig. 1b). It is most important that the join be carefully placed, so that it falls at the fold on the inside. Transfer and embroider the pattern on the right side (fig. 2). Press lightly and sew on the beads. Turn in the raw edges on one side and overcast them together. Do the same with the other side. Lay flat, wrong side uppermost. Cut a piece of vinyl 5½in. × 6¼in. Open the Velcro fastener, which should

Top, The colonel (instructions on p. 85). Square mirror (p. 61). Bottom, Mirror in Thai silk (p. 60). Fanny (p. 84).

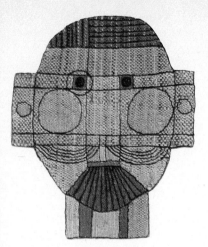

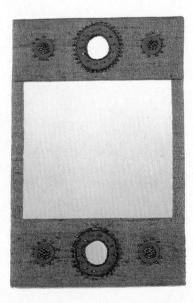

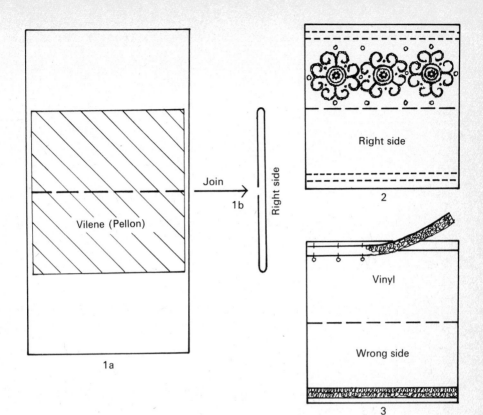

1a

1b

Join

Vilene (Pellon)

Right side

Right side

2

Vinyl

Wrong side

3

be $6\frac{1}{4}$in. long. Pin on the vinyl and the Velcro at the same time. The vinyl will be held down by the Velcro when this is sewn on by machine and should therefore be pinned under it (fig. 3). The vinyl should be stretched a little, i.e. should be a little too short, so as to fit when the pencil case is folded. Cover over the machine seams on the right side with couching. The top line of machining by which the Velcro fastener is attached should be $\frac{1}{4}$in. from the edge. Sew up the short ends by hand from the right side. Take small, close stitches and continue right up to the beginning of the Velcro fastener. See colour illustration facing p. 64.

Dolly (p. 78).

Opening

Theodor

SIZE
10in. × 15¾in.
MATERIALS
mauve-coloured firm
material
wool, or linen threads,
in cerise, orange and
red
wooden beads in
cerise, orange, red and
mauve
STITCH
couching

Cut out two rounds the size you wish the bird to be, allowing an extra ¼in. for turnings. Place them together with the right sides facing and pin all round. Sew round in the sewing machine, the width of the presser foot from the edge, leaving an opening of about 4in. Fasten off the threads by reverse-stitching. Turn inside out. Press. Sew up the opening by hand. Embroider. Sew on the beads except at the edges, so that the bird can be sewn to the background by machine. Cut out two panels measuring 10¾in. × 16½in. Pin the bird on to one of them. Sew down the pocket in the sewing machine. Sew as close to the edge as possible. Leave a large opening at the top, so that, e.g., letters and newspapers can be put into it (see drawing). Fasten off the threads by reverse-stitching. Sew on the remaining beads. Embroider the legs. Turn in and pin the hems of the two background panels. Place them together with the wrong sides facing. Move the pins so that they pass through both layers of material. Sew a hem at the edge in the sewing machine all round. Sew on two metal rings at the back for hanging.
See colour illustration on the front cover.

74

75

Emma

SIZE
9¼in. × 13¼in. (frame)
MATERIALS
mauve, orange and
pink linen
2 mauve sequins for
eyes
bronze-coloured yellow
and pink glass beads
for beak
linen thread in pink,
orange, red and mauve
tape
iron-on Vilene (Pellon)
about 13 yds of brass
wire
brass rings
frame
glue
STITCHES
appliqué
couching
lazy daisy

The background should measure 10in. × 14in. Turn in and tack a hem of ¼in. Cut out the pieces to form the bird, allowing for hem, and iron a piece of Vilene (Pellon) without hem allowance on to the back. Turn in the hems and sew the pieces on to the background. Embroider the eyes, breast and legs in couching and the body with lazy daisy stitch flowers. Sew the beads on to the beak and couch a thread round them. Use a gun stapler to fix the linen to the frame. Cut nineteen lengths of brass wire 24in. long. Bend them at the bottom and roll them up (see drawing). Hold the wires together with a narrow piece of tape. The tape should lie under the wires. Cover the clips with a wider piece of tape. These tapes, each of which has nineteen brass rings sewn on to it, are glued to the front of the frame and sewn to the back. A wide gold thread is stitched over the wires to keep them in place. Brass rings sewn on previously indicate the width of the spaces. Tie the wires together at the top with a short length of brass wire.

See colour illustration facing p. 65.

Dolly

SIZE
16¼in. × 15½in.

MATERIALS
green linen
a different green linen
for appliqué
yellow-green, green
and turquoise
embroidery thread
light and dark green
sequins
green bugle beads and
round beads
brass rings for eyes
iron-on Vilene (Pellon)

STITCHES
shaded stem stitch
couching

Start with a piece of linen 17¼in. × 16½in. Iron a piece of Vilene (Pellon) on to the back. Transfer the pattern to the linen. Then work the wings, head and beak in shaded stem stitch. The bird's body is made of linen of a darker shade. It may be difficult to keep the curved part of the appliqué work even, but it will be a help to iron on a piece of Vilene (Pellon) in the desired shape. The hem can be turned in quite easily when you have a hard outline to follow. Sew on the appliqué pieces with invisible stitches. Press the work from the wrong side. Sew on the sequins and beads. The eyes consist of a large sequin placed under a metal ring. The metal ring is worked round with thread and sewn down. A small bead represents the pupil. This hangs loose from the ring on a double sewing thread.

When the panel is completely finished stretch it face upwards (on account of the sequins) and cover it with a slightly damp cloth. When the cloth is dry the 'pressing' is finished. Turn in the edges of the linen and pin. Tidy up the corners. Then lay the work on a soft surface and iron on two layers of Vilene (Pellon) (because of the size of the panel). Sew on two metal rings for hanging.

See colour illustration facing p. 73.

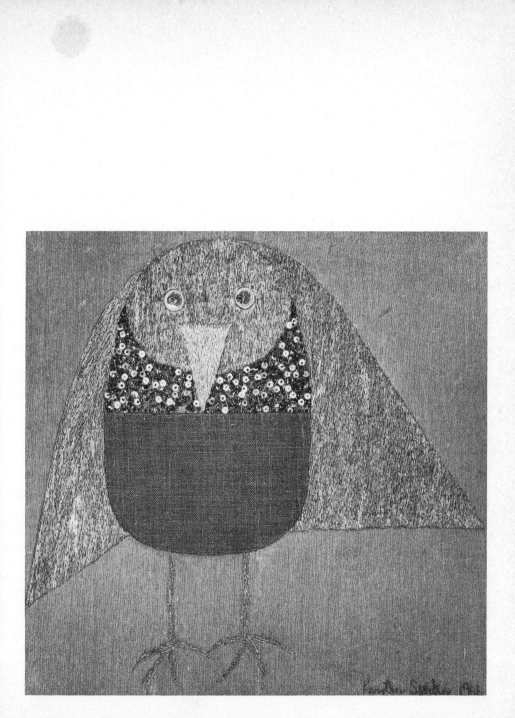

The bridge party

SIZE
11¾in. × 11¾in.
MATERIALS
orange, bluish-mauve,
light mauve and pink
linen
pink, red, mauve and
orange-coloured linen
thread
chipboard (Masonite)
STITCHES
appliqué
couching with double
thread
satin stitch
whirls

The design represents two couples playing cards. The gentlemen have dark, high hats with brims and collars on their shirts. The ladies, in pinker tones, have curly hair and buttons on their blouses. The card symbols indicate that the two couples are playing a game of cards such as bridge.

Overcast the edges of the material (14in. × 14in.) and mark out the centre. Cut out the smaller pieces: two of size 2¾in. × 2¼in. for the gentlemen's hats, two the same size but in a lighter shade for the ladies' hats; eight pieces 1⅜in. × 2⅝in. for the halves of the faces in four different shades of pink, and one piece 2¾in. × 2¾in. for the centre. Cut out the same number of pieces in Vilene (Pellon) but ⅜in. smaller in length and breadth. Iron the Vilene (Pellon) on to the corresponding pieces, keeping it in line with the grain of the material. Turn in the extra ³⁄₁₆in. of material and sew the pieces together by hand from the wrong side, keeping to the line of the weave, to form one connected piece.

Pin this piece to the background, keeping to the line of the weave. Sew it on with invisible stitches. Start at the middle and sew round. First embroider the faces of the ladies and gentlemen, the ladies' hair and the gentlemen's collars in couching. Use double thread for the couching, sewing it down with sewing cotton of exactly the same shade as the linen thread. Then embroider the buttons (whirls – see p. 16), and finally the card symbols, which are worked in satin stitch.

Stretch the embroidery right side up, lay a cloth which has been evenly damped over it and leave until the cloth is dry. Stretch the work over a panel of chipboard (Masonite) and nail it down at the back. Make sure that the corners are neat – one often has to cut away unnecessary material to get it to fold in tidily. Sew a piece of cloth to the back, preferably linen or cotton or the same shade. Drive in a hook for hanging. See colour illustration opposite.

The generations

SIZE
10⅝in. × 14¾in.
MATERIALS
natural-coloured or
unbleached linen
mauve linen for
appliqué
mauve and red tape
mauve, pink, orange,
white and natural
embroidery threads
gold thread
chipboard (Masonite)
STITCHES
stem stitch
French knots
couching
satin stitch
shaded stitch
half cross stitch
lazy daisy stitch
back stitch
Pekinese stitch
appliqué

The generations run from the top left-hand corner, reading vertically downwards. In the first row the priest marries a woman and a man with a moustache. In the fullness of time they have a son. In the next row we find that the family has received the addition of a daughter. The boy is wearing school uniform. The parents hold the family together. In the middle row the boy has left home. The parents remain, at the centre. In the fourth row we see two bridal couples: the children are getting married. We recognize the son by his nose and the daughter by her hair style. She also carries a bridal bouquet similar to her mother's. The last row shows the mother and father with their grandchildren. To illustrate the passage of time there are hour glasses between every row. The last has not yet run out.

The outlines are worked in stem stitch. The hats are made of appliquéd material. The priest's collar is worked in satin stitch, the men's coats and jackets in shaded stem stitch. The bride's crown and the bridal bouquets in satin stitch. The bouquet also contains French knots. The second bouquet contains in addition flowers in lazy daisy stitch. The babies' blankets are embroidered with flowers in lazy daisy stitch or couching with knots or lazy daisy stitch with knots. The father's jacket is made of tape with couching on it. The son's school uniform is embroidered in half cross stitch and back stitch, the grandson's in Pekinese stitch. The spots on the daughter's dress are French knots, as are also the buttons on the mother's. The stripes are worked in stem stitch. The son's pullover is worked in satin stitch; the mother's dress in three layers of tape. The pearl necklace is done in French knots. One half of the hour glass is also filled with French knots. Mount by the same procedure as The Bridge Party (p. 80).

See colour illustration opposite.

The king

All sorts of left-overs of yarn may be used for this. Start with a sketch and give your imagination free play in the weaving. Vary the halves of the face so that they will not look alike. The warp that is over at the top and bottom may, as here, be plaited (braided) and knotted to make the hair or beard. The pupils of the eyes consist of between ten and fifteen beads, depending on size and appearance, threaded on to threads which are fixed in the hair. Fasten off ends of yarn and tape by threading them in or sewing them down with small stitches at the back. Use sewing thread of the same colour as the yarn.

See colour illustration on the back cover.

Detail of weaving.

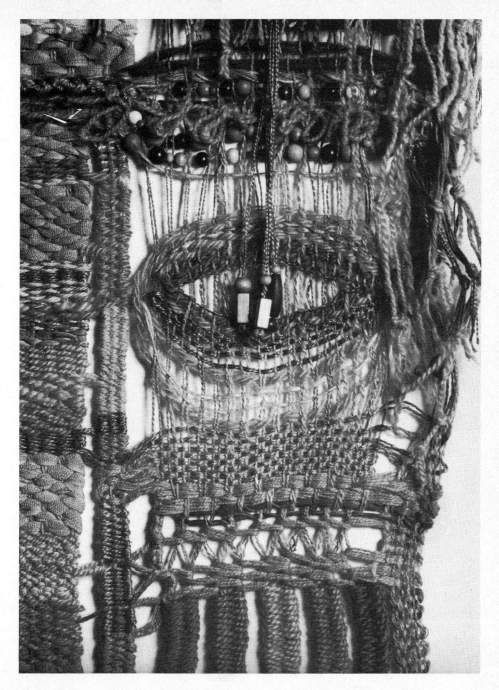

Fanny

SIZE
width, 9⅝in.;
height 10in.
LOOM
toy folding loom
(width of reed 10in.,
density of reed 33/10)
MATERIALS
warp
light brown cotton rug
warp, 84 threads
weft
mauve, blue and brown
fine cotton yarn
light and dark mauve
coarse cotton yarn
brown, mauve and blue
linen thread 16/2
brown and mauve tow
yarn
reddish-brown chenille
yarn
brown string yarn
(divided)
wooden beads in
mauve, brown and red
WEAVING STYLE
Flemish weave

Weave the face from the bottom upwards. Each strand of hair consists of three or four threads, depending on the thickness of the weft. The line of demarcation between the neck and the face is marked by a cord, which is woven in. The eyelashes are made of rug knots. When the face is finished, cut it down. Fasten off the threads by knotting them together two at a time and drawing them through the work for ⅜in.—¾in. At the neck, first knot the threads together two by two. Then thread wooden beads on to the double threads. Make a knot to prevent the beads from slipping off. Sew up any splits except in the forehead.

See colour illustration facing p. 72.

The colonel

SIZE
9¼in. × 10¾in.
REEDS
50/10
MATERIALS
warp
cotton and linen yarns
of different thicknesses
in shades of blue and
brown
weft
coarse cotton yarn,
tow yarn and tapestry
yarn in shades of pink,
rose, pinky mauve
and brown
for embroidery
black cottolin
sewing thread
for mounting
iron-on Vilene (Pellon)
plywood
piece of wood
nails
glue
WEAVING STYLE
Flemish weave

Weave the face in yarns of similar colours in the different parts. Cut out the face allowing a turn-in of about 1¼in. Machine a zigzag stitch round the face. Turn the threads to the back and fasten them off with small stitches all round. Sew up the slits. Embroider the outlines in couching. Iron on two layers of Vilene (Pellon) on to the back. Saw out a face of the same size in plywood or cut it out in thick cardboard. Nail a rectangular piece of wood on to the back with a hole hollowed out or bored through at the centre (for hanging). This should be ⅜in.–¾in. thick in order to hold the face a little away from the wall. Nail from the plywood side. Glue the face on to the wooden board.

See colour illustration facing p. 72.

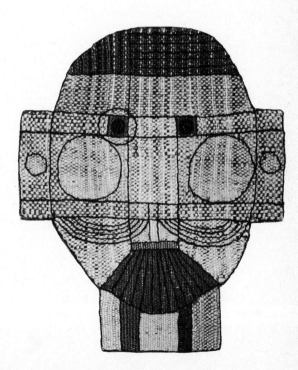

Mali wall ornament

SIZE
3⅝in. × 46¾in.
MATERIALS
warp
black cotton rug warp:
30 threads, 1 thread/
reed space
weft
brown cotton rug warp
brown and black
cottolin yarn
brown and black linen
thread 16/2
pale brown tow yarn
wooden beads
WEAVING STYLE
plain weave ribbing
different kinds of
needleweaving

It will be helpful to work from a sketch, though of course it is not necessary to follow it completely — you should allow yourself a certain freedom. Twisted cords give firmness to the strip, as do also the cotton rug warp in both warp and weft. The beads are threaded on or knotted in only after the strip has been cut down. The warp threads at the top are plaited (braided): five plaits each, consisting of six threads, are sewn together at the top. A ring that has been blanket-stitched round is sewn on at the very top for hanging. At the bottom the warp threads are knotted together, first in small knots of six warp threads each and then a large knot of all the warp threads. The strip is ended off with pink, orange and brown beads.

Day and night

LOOM
(See Fanny, p. 84)
SIZE
8in. × 32in.
MATERIALS
warp
cotton yarn 60 thread
(the yarn is provided
with the loom)
weft
unbleached fancy yarn
chenille yarn
half bleached or
natural linen thread
16/2
brown and black cotton
rug warp
brown tow yarn
silver thread
WEAVING STYLE
Flemish weave

The different types of yarn are used one after another throughout to give the panel an interesting surface. Sometimes the yarns are mixed so that the weft will be double or treble. The sun on the light ground, for example, is in brown and black. The six summer and winter months are also of mixed colours. In two of the winter months one of the components is a thin silver thread. The moon on the dark background is woven of unbleached and half-bleached yarns with two black and silver-coloured threads. The seven days of the week and the nights are also represented underneath the moon. To give a neat finish to the work you can weave it in strips. Each strip contains four threads apart from the first and the last, which contain six threads. The warp threads at the bottom are fastened off by knotting two threads together and drawing them through for $\frac{1}{2}$in.–1in. At the top the weaving is hemmed and three silver-coloured rings are sewn on for hanging.